Stock Market Investing Mini-Lessons For Beginners

Easily digestible and straight to the point mini-lessons on individual stock investing

Mabel A. Nuñez, MBA

Dedications:

God, My higher power – For being my guidance throughout this whole process and beyond.

My awesome parents, Alberto Nunez and Delsi Suriel, as well as my incredible sister, Marlenne Nunez – thank you for always believing in me and my ambitions.

Alimo Noreiga – The person who taught me hands on investing. I am thankful we crossed paths. Thank you for being my answer from the universe and appearing at the perfect time.

The **Girls on The Money** and **Teach Me To Invest** Community – Thank you for allowing me to share my investing knowledge, and what I continue to learn, with all of you.

My editor, Rebekah Groves (beckc_8@hotmail.com) – Thank you for your professionalism, diligence and great work.

Table of Contents:

Part I: Understanding The Stock Market & Individual Stock Investing

Lesson 1: What Is A Stock?	3
Lesson 2: The Difference Between Trading & Investing	5
Lesson 3: How Much Do I Really Need To Start Investing?	7
Lesson 4: The Money That Should Be In The Stock Market {... and what you should keep out}	9
Lesson 5: How Much Of Your Money Should Be In Stocks {Simple Calculation}	11
Lesson 6: Starting An Investing Account	13
Lesson 7: Why Investing Is Like Savings On Steroids	15
Lesson 8: How To Find Your First Stock	17
Lesson 9: What Is An Online Broker/Discount Broker?	18
Lesson 10: Dividends & Dividend Yields	20
Lesson 11: Dividend Payout Ratios	22
Lesson 12: Dividend Aristocrats	23
Lesson 13: The Benefits Of Buying Stocks That Don't Pay Dividends	24
Lesson 14: What Is A Ticker Symbol?	26
Lesson 15: What Are The NYSE And The NASDAQ?	27
Lesson 16: What Makes Stock Prices Go Up Or Down In One Single Day?	28
Lesson 17: What To Do When The Market Is Having a "Down" Day, Week, Month, Year	29
Lesson 18: The Importance Of A Watch List	31
Lesson 19: Mapping Out A Personal Investing Plan {...and why this is important}	33
Lesson 20: If You Can Afford The Product, You Can Afford The Stock	35
Lesson 21: Invest In What You Know, But Take Your Brain With You	37
Lesson 22: What Does It Mean To Buy On Margin? {...and why you should stay away from that}	39

Lesson 23: The Difference Between "Class A" And "Class B" Shares {A clear example using BRK-A and BRK-B}	40
Lesson 24: Penny Stocks	41
Lesson 25: Dollar Cost Averaging (DCA)	43
Lesson 26: How To Invest "Internationally" Without Fear	44
Lesson 27: Top Websites For Investing Research	46
Lesson 28: What Is A Spin-Off?	48
Lesson 29: What Is An IPO?	50
Lesson 30: What Is A 10Q And Why Does It Matter?	51
Lesson 31: Earnings Season	52
Lesson 32: Investors Relations	53
Lesson 33: Annual Reports (10K)	55
Lesson 34: Diversification – What It Is And Why It's Important	57
Lesson 35: Capital Gains Taxes	59
Lesson 36: What Is A Stock Split?	61
Lesson 37: Fundamental Analysis	63
Lesson 38: Technical Analysis	64
Lesson 39: What Is Gross Margin?	65
Lesson 40: Direct Stock Purchase Plans And Transfer Agents: Explained	67
Lesson 41: What Does It Mean To Short A Stock? Is It Worth It?	69
Lesson 42: What Happens When A Stock That You Own Goes "Bankrupt"?	71
Lesson 43: How Long Investors Have To Wait Before Seeing A Return On Stock Investments	74
Lesson 44: When To Sell A Stock	77
Lesson 45: Socially Responsible Investing	79
Lesson 46: How To Prepare Yourself To Start Investing {Five Simple Steps}	81

Part II: Alternate Forms Of Investing (outside of stocks)

1.	ETFs: Exchange Traded Funds	87
2.	Mutual Funds	89
3.	Index Funds	91
4.	Expense Ratios: A General Overview	93

Final Thoughts

© 2016 Mabel A. Nunez. All rights reserved worldwide.

No part of this publication may be reproduced, distributed, or transmitted in any form or by any means, including photocopying, recording, or other electronic or mechanical methods, without the prior written permission of the publisher, except in the case of brief quotations embodied in critical reviews and certain other noncommercial uses permitted by copyright law. For permission requests, send email to: girlsonthemoney@gmail.com. "Attention: Permissions Coordinator".

Disclaimer: Please note that names of publicly traded companies will appear throughout this book and are used as examples to bring educational points across. **Please never invest or cease to invest based solely on the information provided in this booklet.** Always make sure to do your own due diligence!

Notes from the Author

Dear Reader,

This book is a resource specially designed for beginners and individuals with very limited (*if any*) knowledge about the stock market. We will cover everything that you may need to know in order to familiarize yourself with how the stock market works and how you can benefit from it. The book starts at the core of it all – **"what is a stock?"** – and continues on to cover various topics including online brokers and do-it-yourself investing, analyzing individual stocks, building your own personal portfolio and more.

Stock Market investing and educating others on this subject is something that I am extremely passionate about. I aim to dispel any misconceptions around stock investing and show that you don't need to work in Wall Street, have a PhD in Finance, or wear an expensive suit to participate in the stock market. Pretty much anyone who makes a conscious and committed decision to learn this subject can do so and benefit from it.

"If you made it through fifth grade math, you can do it"

With that said, let's dive right in!

Cheers to profits,

Mabel A. Nuñez, MBA

Understanding The Stock Market
&
Individual Stock Investing

Lesson 1:
What Is A Stock?

You can think of a stock as a "piece" of a business. When you buy shares of a publicly traded company, whether it is one single share or a few thousand, you officially become a "part-owner" of that business.

In the old days, when someone purchased stock, they would receive an official "certificate of ownership" which they had to keep filled away at home and carry down to a broker's office if they wanted to sell their position. Today, anyone is able to buy and sell stocks quickly and conveniently from the comfort of their home or anywhere in the world through an online broker (more on this later).

As a shareholder of a publicly traded business, you will benefit from the company's success (i.e. profits) through stock price appreciation and dividend payments – if the company pays dividends. Keep in mind that, although individual investors like you and I can consider ourselves part owners of a business through stock ownership, we don't necessarily have a say on the company's day to day operations. We are basically trusting the management and executives of that particular business to make the best decisions that will generate healthy profits from which we can benefit as shareholders.

One of the main reasons why businesses issue stock to the public is to raise cash in order to improve operations and fund growth strategies for ongoing success. Instead of asking the bank for a loan at high interest rates and complex payment plans, they ask the public to invest in the business in exchange for the company's commitment that executives will do everything in their power for the company to be successful and, in turn, have shareholders benefit over time.

Owning stock also provides shareholders with "limited liability" which means that, if for any reason a company goes out of business, the shareholders cannot lose any more than what they have invested in the company. So, for example, if you own 100 shares in a company that goes bankrupt, all you can lose is whatever the value is for those 100 shares. No one can come after your personal assets. However, there is no ceiling on how much profit you can get from a stock that you own if it continues to be profitable over time – that is one the factors that make investing so exciting.

Lesson 2:
The Difference Between Trading & Investing

Before we continue on this journey of "Mini-Lessons", you should be aware that there are two ways in which you can get involved in the market – as a **trader** or an **investor.**

Trading, in its simplest form, means the constant action of buying and selling stocks and/or other investment securities within short periods of time. Trading is deeply based on technical analysis, which means that it involves understanding charts and patterns while frequently executing trades. The charts that traders look at are created by statistical data based on historical stock prices which may help determine what a stock may do next. Traders go into the market each day with the objective of catching specific trends within a stock chart that would allow them to make a profit in the quickest way possible. Successful traders have to understand what is going on with the patterns that they are following before executing any trades. The trading approach comes with very high levels of risk and speculation and could be especially risky for both beginners and seasoned investors.

***

Investing, on the other hand, is deeply based on fundamental analysis, which means that, instead of buying and selling stocks based on charts and patterns, you focus on the company's fundamentals or its "core" value. For example, an investor makes it a point to look closely at all financial, annual and quarterly statements reported by the company with a special focus on factors that can help determine how successful the company will continue to be. Historical data is no guarantee of future success, but it can help investors make educated decisions about the future and growth prospects of a particular business.

You can think of investing as buying a piece of a company and being a part owner for the long term (i.e.: more than one year and preferably 3-5 years and beyond). When you make the decision to invest in a good company, you will benefit from their growth, their profits and their potential for long-term success. People that invest usually have a long-term goal in mind and look to create wealth over time. Some goals include retirement, a luxurious vacation that you want to take in the future, your kids education, saving up for a future business – the list goes on. When thinking of investing, think "part-owner" and think long-term.

***

The concepts in this book are based primarily on long-term value investing with a strong focus on fundamental analysis which is the method of analyzing the true value of a business through the review of publicly available business documents, financial data, and other factors. All lessons within this booklet will be most relevant to the investor, not the trader.

Lesson 3:
How Much Do I Really Need To Start Investing?

"The journey of one thousand miles begins with one single step."
– Chinese Proverb

Despite popular belief, you don't need much to start investing. Many people are under the impression that you need thousands or "millions" of dollars to begin your investing journey, but that is a huge misconception. There are various online brokers out there today that have no account minimums as well as applications that allow you to invest your spare change or buy partial stocks that come at a lower cost.

In practical terms, a solid ballpark number to start with would be anything from $500 to $1,000. As you become more comfortable with investing, you can move your way up from there and add additional funds to your personal investing account over time and as your budget permits. However, those numbers are not hard and fast rules by any means and can vary depending on the individual. The truth is that investing is very personal and each individual is different so *start* with whatever amount you feel comfortable with.

Once you identify your designated amount, look to start a small portfolio by buying a stock from a few different companies and investing equal amounts on each. For example, let's say you start with $500 – you can look to split that in equal parts and invest in five high-quality stocks. Do the same if you start with $200, $300, or $10,000, etc. You get the point!

You can find amazing stocks out there that sell for less than $100 per share that also pay dividends (*more on dividends later*). Another option that I will talk a bit more about later in the book, you can choose your very first investment to be an index fund or a couple of high-quality index funds. It doesn't always have to be an individual stock.

Below are some **examples** of high-quality stocks that sell for less than $100 a piece. *The stock prices shown are as of December 2015 and may be lower or higher depending on when you are reading this book.*

Starbucks (NASDAQ: SBUX): $60.89
Coca Cola (NYSE: KO): $42
Colgate (NYSE: CL): $65
Procter & Gamble (NYSE: PG): $76
Visa (NYSE: V): $79.20

The stocks are not recommendations, simply examples! Always be sure to do your own due diligence.

Lesson 4:
The Money That Should Be In The Stock Market
{... and what you should keep out}

Two words: **Discretionary Income**

Discretionary income is any income that is left over after you cover all your necessary living expenses: taxes, food, shelter, electricity, insurance, high-interest debt, etc. The money that you have left over after your short-term responsibilities is the money that should be set aside for investing. Money that you need in the short term – think next month, or even within the next few years – should never be in the stock market.

Stock market investing is one of the most efficient ways to build wealth over time. Studies show that, over the last century, large cap stocks have averaged earnings of 10.4% per year. The percentage return is in comparison to long-term government bonds or treasury bills, for instance, which have only appreciated about 5.5% and 3.7% respectively over the same time period.

Regardless of any financially devastating times that we may have faced as a country or within the economy as a whole – from multiple world wars to market crashes and everything in between – the stock market has historically always recovered. With that said, no one ever knows what could happen tomorrow. Market crashes often come without warning and short-term movements within stocks can be volatile and unpredictable. Your investing account should have time to "breathe" and go through its naturally occurring cycles without creating panic that would trigger you to sell because you "need the money".

If we think back to the most recent market crash – the financial crisis of 2008 – many investing accounts suffered losses of up to 50% and beyond. The sad part is not that those accounts decreased in value, but that many people that had money in the market during those times and needed it in the short term panicked and sold their shares. Well, the stock market has recovered more than 150% since that market crash. If those people had just left their money alone, they would have been more than okay today.

If the money that you are setting aside is money that you won't need for some time, you'll have an easier time dealing with the fluctuations of the market and eventually come out ahead. You'll be able to sleep well at night and, instead of panicking, you'll actually be excited for the down times and will learn to look at those downturns as opportunities to accumulate shares of good companies at "discounted" prices.

Lesson 5:
How Much Of Your Money Should Be In Stocks
{Simple Calculation}

While stock market investing can bring huge rewards, it also comes with the caveat of a higher risk in comparison with more "conservative" routes. If you are strategic about the risks that you are taking (i.e. you invest in high-quality companies for the long term), there is not much you have to worry about. However, it is also wise NOT to have 100% of your money solely on stocks. As much as I absolutely love individual stocks, I also understand that the market is volatile and unpredictable. Hence, it is very important to have money outside of the stock market for those "just in case" times, because we just never know.

There is a general rule of thumb for investing and it involves your age and the time horizon your money has to grow and compound. To find what percentage of your investment money should be allocated to individual stocks, simply subtract your current age from 100.

For example, if you are 32 years old, approximately 68% of your money should be in stocks (100-32=68). The rest should be in more liquid/safer kinds of investments – including cash or a money market account – that you can tap into when needed. The general rule of thumb is that the younger you are, the more you should have invested in individual stocks and vice versa.

So, in other words, let's say you have an investing account with $5,000 in it and you are 32 years old. According to the rule, approximately $3,400 out of that $5,000 should be in stocks and "riskier" assets while the rest ($1,600) should be in cash or more liquid assets. This also depends on a person's risk tolerance. So, basically, if you are okay with higher risks (and the possibility of larger rewards over time), you can choose to have a larger percentage of your money in stocks. If your risk tolerance is a bit lower, you can have less in stocks. You get the idea!

The noted theory is based on the time horizon that someone has to be able to tolerate any roller-coaster moments that the stock market decides to have. The closer you are to your retirement years, the less of your money that should be in stocks because, as we get older, we want our money to be as stable and as safe as possible. The farthest you are from retirement, the more time you have for your money to compound over time and the less you have to worry about if anything unpredictable happens in the market.

Lesson 6:
Starting An Investing Account

When you open an online brokerage account (an online broker is a platform where you can buy/sell stocks on your own), the final piece of the application process will be to fund money into the account in order to start investing. The majority of online brokers have no minimum requirement in terms of how much money you can start with. Hence, you can very well fund your account with $10, $100, $10,000 or whatever you can afford and/or feel comfortable with. With that said, before you start investing, it may be a good idea to start an "investing account" (preferably separate from your savings account) where you can accumulate the funds that you exclusively want to use for investing.

You don't need to set aside massive amounts of money to start. I would personally recommend setting aside $20, $30, maybe $50 from every paycheck – the important factor is to stay consistent. If you have online banking, find out if you can set up that separate account and have your bank automatically transfer the funds from every paycheck so that you don't even have to think about it.

I share this with you because this is an approach I personally put into place before I even started investing. While I originally had no knowledge of the stock market, I knew one of my goals would be to invest one day. And so, I set money aside for that purpose alone. Once I was finally ready to embark on my investing journey, I was able to use the funds that I had saved to purchase my very first stock.

Remember, you can start with saving whatever amount you feel comfortable with and then work your way up from there. Or, you may already have a lump sum set aside. In which case, consider adding to that fund bi-weekly, monthly, or as often as you possibly can. You'll be glad that you did. The more money that you are able to set aside for investing, the more choices you'll have in terms of which companies to invest in and how many shares you'll be able to buy.

Lesson 7:
Why Investing Is Like Savings On Steroids

If you have followed my investing style for some time, you may have noticed how much I emphasize the importance of **long-term value investing.** I strongly believe that investing for the long term is one of the best ways that we can create wealth over time. Quality investing should not be seen as a "get rich quick scheme", as buying and selling stocks within short periods of time can be very risky and costly.

One of the traits that motivates me the most about long-term value investing is the fact that we can make our money work hard for us. By investing in high-quality companies at the right time, we can benefit from their continuous growth over time and continue building our wealth in the process. We can benefit from both price appreciation and dividend payments where applicable. As outlined in lesson 4, money in an investing account generally has the potential to grow a lot faster than the money sitting in a savings account that's getting less than pennies on the dollar. The average interest rate on a savings account these days is around 0.01% while returns in an investing account can be exponential.

Don't get me wrong, I am a strong believer in savings and agree that we should ALL have money set aside for emergencies that is easily accessible and not tied to investments. The truth of the matter is that we never know what could happen. However, having an investing account is just as important if we wish to grow our wealth more efficiently.

Below are some examples and proof of why I say that investing is like savings on steroids. Let's take a closer look at the performance of some well-known companies over the past five years (*none of these are recommendations. They are simply examples for this particular lesson*).

Amazon
Stock Price 10/09/2010: 155.55
Stock Price 10/09/2015: 539.80
Percentage Increase: 247%

Disney
Stock Price 10/09/2010: 32.07
Stock Price 10/09/2015: 105.56
Percentage Increase: 229%

L Brands (Parent company of Victoria Secret, Bed Bath & Beyond, La Senza)
Stock Price 10/09/2010: 20.63
Stock Price 10/09/2015: 96.34
Percentage Increase: 366%

*All of the above companies (with the exception of Amazon) pay a dividend. The percentage gains shown don't include the dividend payments, which means that the return on investment for each of the above is actually more than illustrated.

Keep In Mind: #1 these gains did not happen overnight. The analysis takes into account percentage increase in stock price over the last **five years**. Money in the stock market should never be money that you need in the short term. You must allow the money to grow. **#2** we've been enjoying a very profitable "bull market" since the financial crisis of 2008 and this has been reflected in many companies across the board.

Lesson 8:
How To Find Your First Stock

Hint: It's a lot easier than you think.

When it comes to investing in your ***first*** stock, you don't have to over-complicate yourself! The fact of the matter is that solid investing ideas can be found pretty much everywhere. If you look around your own home, your place of work, the websites that you use, the places where you frequently shop etc., you can likely find your first high-quality idea for stocks(s) that will propel you into your long-term investing journey.

As you go about your life, pay very close attention to your surroundings. Look at companies and brands that are highly popular and acclaimed by people that you know or even strangers – these can provide some great ideas. Once you have identified a company that catches your attention, add it to your watch list and start your research *(more on this later)*! Some questions/ideas to get you thinking:

1. What brand of toothpaste do you use? How long have you used that brand? Who makes it?
2. What is your beverage of choice on a hot summer's day? Who makes it?
3. What kind of phone do the vast majority of your friends have?
4. What website do you use the most for online shopping or for searches?
5. What is the brand of your face/body lotion/shampoo?
6. What kind of car do you drive? Would you recommend it? Who makes it?

...Can you identify some ideas?

Lesson 9:
What Is An Online Broker/Discount Broker?

Once upon a time – not too long ago actually – if you wanted to buy/sell stocks, you'd have to walk down to some fancy office or call up a broker that had the authority and credentials to complete the transaction for you. Those brokers usually charged hundreds of dollars simply to buy or sell shares of a stock for you, using *your* money. Thankfully, those days are long gone and we have a lot more accessible (and affordable) options.

Today, you can open your own brokerage account online (*also known as a discount or online broker*), fund it with your own money and buy individual stocks yourself. The costs are significantly low. For example, most well known online brokers today charge anywhere from $4.95 to $9.99 per trade on average. Using the $4.95 example, this means that every time you buy shares in a company in bulk (it doesn't matter how many shares you buy), they will charge you $4.95. Whenever you decide to sell the share(s), they will charge you $4.95 again.

So, for example, if you made a profit of $1,000 on a stock and you decide to sell your position. Your only fees for that buy/sell transaction to the online broker will be $9.90 (*4.95x2=9.90*), leaving you with a profit of $990.01 (not counting taxes) ... Quite a nice deal, right?

Some of the most popular online brokers today include TDAmeritrade, TradeKing, E*Trade, ScotTrade, Capital One Investing, First Trade – the list goes on! There are numerous options out there including several up-and-coming phone apps and online applications that invest on your behalf, based on your risk tolerance, completely free of charge.

As a general rule of thumb, remember this – when choosing an online broker, make sure that they are insured by **SIPC** (Security Investor Protection Corporation) – this is a branch of the U.S. government which is in charge of regulating online brokerage accounts and making sure that they are in compliance. Just like the FDIC protects your checking and savings account, the SIPC protects your online brokerage investing account. Always make sure to look for the SIPC logo when choosing an online broker (see below):

Source

Lesson 10:
Dividends & Dividend Yields

Dividends are a portion of a company's earnings that are paid to shareholders (individuals that own the stock) once a year, twice a year, or most commonly – every three months (quarterly). You can think of dividends as something akin to an interest rate that you get from a bank – only better!

You don't have to do absolutely anything to get this money other than to own at least one share of a stock that pays a dividend. Companies do this in order to reward shareholders. So, the more successful and profitable the company becomes, the more the people that own the stock can benefit – not only from the price appreciation in the actual stock, but from getting dividends (which some companies tend to raise every year). Getting these "double perks" make dividend-paying stocks my favorite.

Example:
Let's say you own **100** shares of Nike (NKE). Their current dividend (as of December 2015) is $1.12 per share with a yield of 1.10%. This means that you get an extra $112 per year or $28 in your account every 3 months in dividend payments. The company simply deposits the money in your brokerage account and you can use that money to buy more shares of Nike, buy something else, or simply leave it there until your next investing opportunity arises.

For another example, let's say you own **100** shares of McDonalds (MCD). The company pays $3.40 per share annually (yield of 3.50%). In this case, you get an extra $340 per year or $85 every three months in dividend payments. Again – this is passive income; you don't have to do anything other than owning shares to get it.

Notice that the amount of dividends you get is directly tied to how many shares of the stock you own and the respective dividend yield.

Note that not all companies pay a dividend. An easy way to find out is by going to a site like Dividend Investor (http://www.dividendinvestor.com/), typing in the name of the company (ticker symbol) and all the dividend information should be available.

You can also go to Yahoo! Finance (Finance.Yahoo.Com), type in the name of the company/ticker symbol and look for "dividend/yield" within the information page of the stock. If it says **N/A,** it usually means the stock doesn't pay a dividend.

Did you know: Some people strategically plan their portfolio around dividend-paying stocks with the goal of one day being able to retire and live off those dividend payments?! This is what is known as a "dividend investor".

Lesson 11:
Dividend Payout Ratios

As noted, dividend payments come from a company's profits. In order to reward shareholders, management looks to allocate a portion of those earnings to give something "extra" back to the individuals that own the stock. Many high-quality well-known companies have historically raised dividends on a yearly basis.

In order for a company to continue growing and being profitable, it can't possibly return all its earnings to shareholders in the form of dividends. They have to keep funds within the company in order to invest in further growth and development and to continue benefiting shareholders over time.

One of the things you should look into when figuring out whether a company's dividend is sustainable is their **"Dividend Payout Ratio" (DPR).** A healthy dividend payout ratio, by rule of thumb, is about 60%. This means that, while the business may be returning 60% of earnings back to shareholders, they are keeping about 40% in-house to fund further growth. A dividend payout ratio of 90% or 100% and beyond should be a red flag. This means that they don't have much money left over to invest back into the business. Or, even worse, if the dividend payout ratio is above 100%, it may mean that the business may be borrowing money to pay dividends which should never be the case.

You can easily calculate the DPR by using this formula:

DPR=Yearly Dividends per Share/Earnings per Share

Or, you can simply look it up online. A couple of great websites that I personally use to find dividend payout ratios are dividendinvestor.com or Morningstar.com

Lesson 12:
Dividend Aristocrats

Dividend aristocrats are companies that have been **paying and increasing dividends for at least 25 years or longer**. These types of companies have been confronted with everything from world wars (*sometimes more than one*), multiple market crashes and various world-disasters. However, they have continued paying shareholders a quarterly dividend regardless of the circumstances. They have also continued to increase them in the process, as mentioned.

As you have learned so far, dividend-paying stocks offer you the "double benefit" of not only profiting when the stock price goes up, but they also pay you every 3 months (on average) simply from owning the stock. dividend aristocrats have proven themselves by showing investors that, regardless of the circumstances, they will continue rewarding them.

Below are examples of some "dividend aristocrats" that you may recognize and the number of years they have been paying dividends:

Procter & Gamble {58 years}
Johnson & Johnson {52 years}
Coca-Cola {52 years}
Colgate-Palmolive {51 years}
Pepsi Co Inc {42 years}
Clorox {37 years}

Lesson 13:
The Benefits Of Buying Stocks That Don't Pay Dividends

This is a question that I personally asked myself when I first started buying stocks. In a nutshell, when a company doesn't pay dividends it could mean that **#1** they are still in the middle of an "aggressive" growing phase and don't have the funds to pay dividends, or **#2** they are, in fact, very profitable but are using any extra cash to continue growing and funding projects that will benefit shareholders for years to come.

Companies that pay dividends are usually those companies that are well established, mature and aren't growing as much as they used to anymore. Think of it as companies that have achieved more of a "revenue maintenance" status.
Companies like Colgate, Coca-Cola and Procter & Gamble are perfect examples. Although these businesses still strive for growth and development, their brand power is so strong and established that they can afford to give more back to investors as opposed to a business that is still growing aggressively.

A perfect example of a company that doesn't pay dividends but has offered great value to shareholders over the years is **Alphabet Inc.** (NASDAQ: GOOGL), better known as Google. As of December 2015, this company has about $70 billion worth of cash and short-term investments on its balance sheet. Instead of paying it to shareholders, they are using it to fund projects not only for their core business (being a search engine) but also for the future – think Google cars, contact lenses for diabetics, space ship projects –the list goes on. If the company continues to be as successful as it has been, shareholders will be happy about not collecting dividends, knowing that the money is going towards projects that will benefit them in the long term. One share of Google currently trades for well over $700 per share (*price as of

December 2015). The stock price has increased by over 44% in 2015 alone.

Lesson 14:
What Is A Ticker Symbol?

You may have noticed that, when I write the name of a company, I usually place an abbreviation next to it. For example, Nike (NKE), Disney (DIS), Coca-Cola (KO) and Apple (AAPL). The abbreviation that you are seeing is called a "ticker symbol" and is the "name" under which publicly traded companies are presented in the stock market.

When you are buying/selling stocks within an online brokerage account, you have to use the ticker symbol in order to make your transaction. It is very easy to find a company's ticker symbol. You can simply Google the phrase "[company] ticker symbol" or go to Yahoo! Finance and type in the business name in the search bar. Keep in mind that only publicly traded companies have ticker symbols.

Lesson 15:
What Are The NYSE And The NASDAQ?

The NYSE (New York Stock Exchange) and the NASDAQ (National Association of Securities Dealers Automated Quotations) are exchanges where the vast majority of publicly traded stocks in North America and worldwide choose to trade. In other words, these are the locations where public companies decide to "house" their shares for trading/investing.

Historically speaking, the NASDAQ houses the vast majority of technology and e-commerce companies including Apple, Google and Amazon to name a few. The New York Stock Exchange houses more traditional businesses and companies geared towards consumer goods and services such as food companies, financial companies, manufacturing, etc. – think Procter & Gamble, Coca-Cola, Goldman Sachs and 3M. The NYSE is also an older exchange as it was established in 1817 while the NASDAQ was created in 1971.

Lesson 16:
What Makes Stock Prices Go Up Or Down In One Single Day?

One Word: *Volume* – which is market lingo for the amount of buying or selling activity generated by institutional investors.

In a nutshell, institutional investors include individuals that manage huge pools of money such as mutual funds and endowments and trade stocks at significantly larger quantities in comparison to an individual investor. For this reason, institutional investors usually have the power to move the direction of stocks in one single day. If smaller quantities of a particular stock are sold off, this makes the stock price go down. On the other hand, if stocks are bought in great quantities, this makes the stock price go up. Remember supply and demand from your economics class? That's very similar to what happens in the market and what contributes to stock price fluctuations.

Furthermore, any type of **macro**economic factors such as any conflicts regarding economic, financial or political issues around the world, news from the Federal Reserve, interest rate news and multiple other factors can trigger stock prices to go up or down. These are all *temporary* situations that come with the territory of investing in the stock market. Markets around the world are very closely connected these days, and so, any turmoil that's going on in other major economies including Europe, China or developing countries, can also have an effect in the U.S. market.

Lesson 17:
What To Do When The Market Is Having A "Down" Day, Week, Month, Year

If the only constant in this life is change, then the only constant in the stock market is volatility. For as long as the stock market has been in existence, it has always fluctuated for various reasons – from international turmoil to domestic economic issues and everything in between. The stock market is not immune to what happens around the world, whether positive or negative, and you will see this reflected quite often in the unexpected movements that you will notice. Sometimes you will also notice the media looking to instill panic among investors for one reason or another. This is why it is so important to educate ourselves and understand how the market works so that misinformation doesn't get the best of us. With that said, one of the concepts that you should be aware of is "market correction".

A *correction* happens when an entire stock market index goes down by 10% or more. The most recent correction that we have experienced (for a very brief period of time) was during the summer of 2015 when the Dow Jones Industrial Average decreased by 10.1%. Along with the Dow Jones, other major indexes also decreased significantly including the S&P 500 and the NASDAQ. The drop across the board hadn't been experienced since 2011. It is also possible that, by the time you are reading this book, we may have experienced other corrections. The decline in 2015 was partly a result of the Chinese slowing economy which also contributed to declines in the European Market. As you will come to understand, all markets around the world are deeply connected.

Corrections or similar types of situations should not worry us as long-term value investors. I'd go as far as saying that they should actually make us excited.

A long-term value investor (someone that plans to hold their stocks for 3-5 years and beyond) doesn't worry about temporary setbacks in the stock market. Whether the setback lasts 1 week or 1 year, we should always remember that we are in this for the long term. And thus, there should be no reason to panic. Ever since the market was created these types of "market downturns" have occurred at various levels of severity and the market has historically always bounced back.

This is why it is also important to remember that any money you allocate to the stock market should not be needed on a short-term basis. People who trade for a living (especially those who buy and sell consistently in one single day) run the risk of being caught up in devastating times when the market suffers unexpected significant losses. Imagine being in the middle of a trade with thousands of dollar on the line. I wouldn't even want to imagine what happens to traders in those circumstances.

And so, whenever you notice the market acting chaotic, do yourself a favor and **don't panic.** Try not to look at your portfolio if you can until the "storm" passes and/or try being strategic and take a look at the companies on your watch list – are any of the stocks on that list "on sale"? A significant downturn in the overall market may be a good time to pick up some shares. With that said, always make sure that you always do your due diligence and confirm that the drop in the stock price is related to what is going on in the market as a whole and not as a result of internal issues within the company.

Remember this: The market fluctuates. Always has and always will. If you want to be an active participant of the stock market, you have to come to terms with that. Thankfully, the good times tend to stay with us longer.

Lesson 18:
The Importance Of A Watch List

When people ask me what the very first thing that they should do when starting their investing journey is, I tell them to start their own personal watch list – a list of companies that they may be interested in and which they can reference when they are finally ready to make their first investment.

I started investing right in the middle of the financial crisis of 2008 when the stock market and financial world as we knew it was "falling apart". Instead of becoming fearful of the stock market, I actually became very excited. I took a good look at my watch list and was happy to see that the prices of many of the stocks I had on that list had been cut down by 30%, 40%, 50% and beyond. I felt motivated to get started and actually started building my portfolio right in the middle of those "devastating" times.

You don't need to wait for a market crash or financial turmoil to start your investing journey, but you do have to be aware of what kind of businesses or companies you want to become a shareholder of when you are ready to do so.

The moral of this story: **keep a watch list!**

Carry a notebook or piece of paper around in your wallet or purse and start writing down the names of fabulous companies that you may come across or may be interested in. Once you have a list of about ten companies, start doing some research (more on this later) and start keeping and/or eliminating companies based on your findings.

Remember: Never invest out of fear or panic –take your time to learn and gather information. Never feel like you are missing out on anything. The stock market isn't going anywhere. If you have a watch list handy, you will always be "ready to go" when the ideal time for you arrives. *Start that list today!*

Lesson 19:
Mapping Out A Personal Investing Plan
{...and why this is important}

Having an investing plan is important because it can help ease any kind of worries and anxieties that you may have when it comes to investing. As with many things in life, having a set plan and objective can help guide us and remain focused as we work towards our ultimate goals. Your general investing plan should include the following:

Objective: Your personal goals for investing – why are you doing it? What is your time horizon? How long do you plan to hold your shares for?

Watch List Criteria: What qualities are you looking for when analyzing individual companies? Do you have a preference for a particular industry or sector? Do you want companies that are already well known and established or would you prefer up-and-coming start-ups that appear to have some good long-term potential? Maybe you want your portfolio to include businesses of low and high risks or perhaps you prefer only dividend-paying stocks. These are just some factors to think about.

Entry Rules: What is your plan for buying shares? How many shares would you feel comfortable with buying from a particular company and at what price?

Money Management: What percentage of your portfolio will you allocate to each stock? For example, do you want to have 20% of your money in Coca-Cola and 50% in Apple, or vice versa? Do you want your investments to be equally divided? This can all depend on your risk tolerance.

Exit Rules: What will be your criteria for selling shares? Which factors are deal breakers in your personal investing portfolio?

Routine: How often will you buy stocks? Bi-Weekly? Monthly? Yearly? Whenever the opportunity presents itself?

It's important to sit down and map out a plan early on in your investing journey. You'll be able to go back and study your original plan whenever the market is going crazy and you aren't sure what to do. It is something I personally do and, trust me, it helps!

Lesson 20:
If You Can Afford The Product, You Can Afford The Stock

Take a second and let this statement marinate in your mind for a bit:

Businesses are made up of consumers, employees and investors – you have the power to choose your role.

There is no denying that most of us (and I include myself) have our "consumer hats" on most of the time whenever we go out into the world. However, as prospective investors, it is important to keep our eyes and minds open to understanding that, if we can spend hundreds (or even thousands) of dollars on a particular product or service, we can probably also afford to own a piece (or several "pieces") of that company.

Consider the following Examples:

- With the cost of one single iPhone 6 plus (at their current retail price of $749) you can buy yourself about 6 shares of Apple stock. *One single share of **AAPL** is currently trading at $115.*
- With the cost of one Starbucks beverage per week for a year (at an average price of $5 per visit, which would come out to around $260 per year), you can buy yourself 4 shares of Starbucks stock. *One share of **SBUX** is currently trading at $60.*
- With the cost of a pair of the most recent Jordan's (at a cost of about $200), *you can buy a share of Nike. **NKE** is currently trading at about $128 per share.*
- With the cost of a $1 bottle of Coca-Cola five days a week for a year (which would come out to around $240 per year), you can buy yourself 5 shares of Coca-Cola stock. ***KO** is currently trading at about $42 per share.*

*Prices noted above are as of December 2015.

So there you have it! Next time you go on a shopping spree and pick up a few items, take a second to ask yourself whether the item that you are holding is publicly traded and whether you'd rather buy the stock instead (or both).

Don't get me wrong, I love having nice things as much as the next person and I believe it is important and awesome to be able to treat ourselves from time to time and enjoy the money that we work so hard for. The point I am trying to make here is that if sometimes you feel that you cannot participate in the stock market because you "can't afford it", please keep this in mind: **"If you can afford the product, you can afford the stock".**

PS: It is also important to remember that not all great products or services make great investments, which that brings us to our next lesson.

*The noted companies are simply examples, not recommendations.

Lesson 21:
Invest In What You Know, But Take Your Brain With You

Let's take a trip down memory lane as I'd like to share one of my favorite examples when it comes to this particular topic. Remember the days when the company Blockbuster Video had some kind of undeclared monopoly when it came to video rentals? A company like Blockbuster had such strong brand power and popularity that the idea of anything ever replacing its status within the industry of family entertainment probably never crossed our minds.

Meanwhile, something was brewing in the world of technology that would not only wipe out Blockbuster in its entirety but would start disrupting other industries, such as the world of cable. You can likely guess what company I am talking about – that company is Netflix. The business is up over 2000% since 2004:

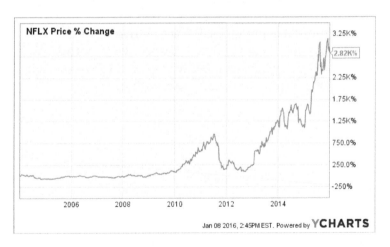

Meanwhile, the original blockbuster (as we knew it) is no longer in existence.

The point that I am trying to make here is that we should always take a serious look at the companies we are considering for long-term value investing. One of the main things to keep a VERY close eye on is competition and how fierce that competition may be.

It is VERY possible for a company to remain #1 for many years, decades, even centuries! However, there is always that "competition" risk that we have to keep an eye on. If you start to notice that your original investing thesis for buying a stock is changing rapidly, you are no longer comfortable with where the company is headed and there is hard-to-ignore aggressive competition on the horizon, then that should be your sign to take a deeper dive into what may be going on. You can decide for yourself whether it may be time to move on or whether the status of that particular business is too strong to be replaced.

An educated, informed and well-aware investor is a successful investor. Investing in what we know and understand is one of the best techniques that we have to become profitable investors. We are motivated to keep on top of those businesses and their respective performance over time. However, remember to stay alert to unexpected changes and always take your brain with you.

Lesson 22:
What Does It Mean To Buy On Margin?
{...and why you should stay away from that}

When you open an online brokerage account, you will notice that the online broker will give you the option of a "margin account".

Buying on margin means that the online broker lends you money to buy stocks and also gives you a set amount of time to pay them back. The VERY dangerous side of buying on margin is that the online broker will not care whether or not you have made money with your investment. Furthermore, borrowing on margin comes with interest involved, some as high as 9% or more. Investing on margin is extremely risky, especially for beginner investors just starting to learn. You never want to be in a position where, instead of making a profit in the market, you now owe your online broker thousands of dollars.

Moral of the story: never invest with borrowed money. As we have learned so far – the market can be very unpredictable. You never want your investments to depend on someone else. You want to be able to sleep well at night with no worries. There is no better feeling! So, when the discount brokerage application asks whether you'd like a margin account, click NO and move on.

Lesson 23:
The Difference Between "Class A" And "Class B" Shares.
{A clear example using BRK-A and BRK-B}

Some companies have what are called **"Class A shares"** and **"Class B shares"**. The only differences between the two types are the voting rights and who is able to own each type of shares. One of the main reasons that companies do this is to make sure that the majority of the decision-making power stays in-house with the owners of the company. It helps avoid the risk that outside investors with a lot of money (i.e. activist investors) come in and buy tons of shares allowing them to have too much power over decision making within the business.

One prime example of where you will see Class A shares and Class B shares are with the company **Berkshire Hathaway Inc**. (owned by one of the most important investors of our time, Warren Buffet).

- One share of the Class A category currently trades at $201,520 (yes, one single share)

- One share of the Class B category trades at $134.57, making it more accessible to individual investors.

Prices as of December 2015

It is important to keep in mind that, even if you owned one share of Class A, you still wouldn't be able to show up at the offices of Berkshire Hathaway and demand your own rules. The average investor doesn't have much say on a company's operations.

Lesson 24:
Penny Stocks

There is no way to sugar coat how I feel about these investments – please stay away, your hard earned money deserves better. Penny stocks are speculative and unsecured types of investments that trade at $5 or less but most commonly at less than $1. Often times these are companies you have never heard of before and/or may have a hard time understanding exactly how they generate profits (if they do at all).

As you will learn later in the lessons, all publicly traded companies are required by law to submit annual reports, quarterly reports, multiple financial reports and all types of disclosures to the public on a fairly consistent basis. One of the reasons why penny stocks can be of a high risk is because they don't have those kinds of requirements.

While some penny stocks may actually be legitimate companies, you can also find many examples of fraud involving those types of investments. Someone can easily come up with a random ticker symbol, hype up the "stock", have people buy shares and then that same person can sell all their shares at a profit leaving everyone else up in arms. If you are going to invest your hard earned money, make sure you go for legitimate companies that have public information available.

Another important factor to remember is that the SEC (Security Exchange Commissions) – the government entity that regulates investments – offers no protection or guarantees if anything happens with a penny stock.

In summary, here are the top three reasons to stay away from Penny Stocks:

1. Penny stocks are NOT regulated by the Security Exchange Commission (SEC). If your investment disappears right in front of your eyes after thinking that you were going to make a million dollars, you are very much on your own.

2. All legitimate publicly traded companies are required to submit annual reports, quarterly reports, financial statements and other business related documents to the SEC on a quarterly basis. Penny stocks are not tied to any of those requirements, nor do they provide them. The ones that do are providing documents that are usually not audited and not regulated by authorities.

3. You have no accurate way of knowing the company's history, how the company is performing, or how it will perform in the future. There is basically no blueprint to know what could happen to your money.

Lesson 25:
Dollar Cost Averaging (DCA)

Dollar Cost Averaging is a technique where you invest in a particular stock or business over a period of time rather than all at once. It allows you to pick up shares at the highs and lows and end up with a fairly valued average price over a specified time horizon. For example, let's say you have **$500** to invest in a company that today costs **$25 per share** and you are trying to decide whether to buy all your shares at once or spread out buying shares over time.

- Let's say that today, the price is $25

- A month from today, the stock is $22

- The following month, the stock is $21

- The next month, the stock goes up to $30

So, if you decide to "spread out" your money and invest on the same day every month, you will end up having shares at a "cheaper" average price of **$24.50** per share as opposed to **$25** or **$30** per share. The technique creates discipline and can help you minimize the risk of buying a stock too high.

Considering that the stock market is always fluctuating and we never know exactly what will happen from one day to the next, **Dollar Cost Averaging** allows us to pick up shares at various prices – sometimes a little low, sometimes a little high. This type of technique can help some investors feel more confident and comfortable with buying shares and can help prevent making purchases out of emotion or hype in the market.

Lesson 26:
How To Invest "Internationally" Without Fear

When we think about "investing internationally", we may be under the impression that we have to blindly put our money in companies that we don't even know. Many of us forget that we can very well have international businesses in our stock portfolios by simply looking into companies that not only have operations in North American but also ALL over the world.

Many companies that we know very well do business all over the world. Some of these companies include McDonald's (**MCD**), Coca-Cola (**KO**) and Colgate (**CL**) just to name a few. For example, did you know that over 80% of Colgate sales actually take place outside of the U.S.?! That's the case for many other companies that we are well familiar with.

- To find out whether a business that you have an interest in has an international presence, simply go to the "investor relations" section of their website and click around for "locations". Check out what countries you see there (if any) and you can also confirm whether the business only has operations in the U.S.
- Another way to find out is to browse through the company's annual report for said information. Also, whenever you travel abroad, look at your surroundings and notice whether you can spot any "American" companies around you. Take some time to ask the locals whether those businesses are popular or what they think of them.

Although I absolutely love the idea of investing in companies that do business all over the world, there are pros and cons which we need to keep in mind.

The Pros: Companies with international operations don't simply have to rely on their performance in North America for profits and customers. These companies have the luxury of having multiple sources of income from various places. Hence, if there is trouble in one country or continent, they can depend on other parts of the world for results. As with everything else, diversification helps in lowering the amount of risk.

The Cons: Some of the cons include foreign exchange rates and having to deal with rules and regulation from a different type of government. In the case of exchange rates, 2015 was a year in which the value of the dollar went up in comparison to other currencies around the world. Well, this may sound good but it also means that the value of other currencies decreased relative to the dollar. Hence, when it comes time to report revenues from other places of the world, companies with international presence may have to report "lower" revenues because of that devaluation. The governments in certain countries are also known to give American companies a hard time when it comes to collecting all of their revenue and may impose heavy taxation in order to compel those businesses to stay in their respective country.

In conclusion, being invested in companies that you know well but have operations abroad can be a good way to participate internationally without much risk. However, it is important to weigh the pros and cons to see whether you are comfortable with the caveats that come with that, as noted above.

*companies noted in this lesson are examples, not recommendations.

Lesson 27:
Top Websites For Investing Research

While there are tons of amazing and highly valuable resources online for investors, I usually stick to a selected group of specialized sites. Some of my top picks include the following:

<u>Investors Relations</u>: ALL publicly traded companies have an Investors Relations section of their website. In that section, you will be able to find ALL annual reports, quarterly reports, press releases on how the company is doing and anything else related to the growth and development of the company that you are doing research on.

<u>Yahoo! Finance</u>: This website has been the #1 go-to in the investing world for as long as I can possibly remember. The individual stock pages provide an overview of pretty much any data that you may be looking for when analyzing a business.

<u>Morningstar</u>: This site offers pretty much the same data you can find on Yahoo! Finance but goes a step further by providing more in-depth information in regards to various metrics and additional data. This site allows the user to find more advanced tools such as ratios and valuation information that may not be readily available on Yahoo! Finance. They offer a paid service as well but the free resources are just as valuable.

<u>Dividend Investor</u>: I love dividend-paying stocks and this website provides very specific information about the companies that pay dividends to shareholders. They include the year that the company started paying dividends, how often they pay it, dividend yield information and more!

<u>Investopedia:</u> Sometimes, when I am analyzing companies, I come across financial terms and other data that I may not be clear on what it means. Investopedia can be thought of as an "investing dictionary" and has been my go-to for investing terminology for a very long time.

<u>Seeking Alpha:</u> In this site, you will find various articles and analyst reports regarding pretty much any stock(s) that you may be considering. You can think of it as an informative platform where multiple analysts and investing enthusiasts come together to present their research and points of view about the prospects of a particular business to help investors make informative decisions.

<u>Motley Fool:</u> A great resource for beginner investors. When I first started my investing journey, I would read articles from the Motley Fool to familiarize myself with investing concepts and strategies. What I love about the Motley Fool is that they do a great job simplifying investing news and anything that may be going on with a particular business. It was probably my first resource for investing education.

Lesson 28
What Is A Spin-Off?

In a nutshell, a spin-off happens when a big corporation makes the decision to separate one of its divisions and make it into its own stand-alone, independent company. Many corporations do this in order to have a better focus on their operations. They may also feel that separating a particular subdivision into an independent company with its own management and operations may be much more successful and efficient in the long run.

When a part of a business separates in this manner, they operate as a stand-alone company with their own ticker symbol.

Below are a few interesting spin-offs over the years:

- **Mondelez International (MDLZ):** This is the parent company of Oreo cookies, Chips Ahoy and other famous goodies. Mondelez was once part of Kraft Foods (now Kraft-Heinz – KHC). This spin-off was completed in October 2012.

- **Chipotle (CMG):** Did you know that Chipotle was once owned by McDonalds (MCD)? The Chipotle business debuted as its own company in 2006 and has become a massive and incredibly successful business. One share of Chipotle currently trades at $561 v. $113 for one share of McDonalds (*prices as of December 2015*).

- **PayPal (PYPL):** For many years Paypal and Ebay (EBAY) were one single company until just recently when Ebay management decided that it would be best to split the company in two and make PayPal its own stand-alone operation. Paypal separated from Ebay in June 2015.

Lesson 29:
What Is An IPO?

IPO, also known as Initial Public Offering, is what the investment world calls companies that go from being private to public for the very first time. When a company is private, the average person can't own any shares in it (only the owners of the company and/or private investors can benefit). However, once a company becomes public, individual investors like you and I can buy a piece of it. Some of the most popular companies that launched IPOs in 2015 include Etsy (NYSE: ETSY), Fitbit (NYSE: FIT) and Shake Shack (NASDAQ: SHAK).

A warning about IPOs: Never, ever, ever invest in IPOs on the first day that they come out and preferably not for another 12-24 months after the company has become public. Some investors may not agree with me, but here is the thing – most of the reasons why shares of IPOs go up in price the first day of trading is due to the excitement and the hype in Wall Street (investing can be extremely psychological). It may have nothing to do with the true intrinsic value of a business. When you invest in an IPO right away, you run the risk of buying at a very high price only to see the value of that stock continually decrease as the days go by. By being patient and waiting things out, you'll save yourself a lot of headaches and frustrations.

Lesson 30:
What Is A 10Q And Why Does It Matter?

A 10Q is also known as a "quarterly report". One of the requirements of being a publicly traded company is that every three months, the business is required to provide a status to the SEC (Securities & Exchange Commission) and shareholders advising them of the company's performance. You can think of it as similar to a "report card" from companies to the public.

If you think about it, a simple three months can't necessarily make or break a company. Hence, if a company you invested in perhaps didn't do so well one quarter, this doesn't mean that you should panic and sell. Your decision to sell or buy should be based on the overall core of the business and its performance.

This is why being a long term value investor is so important – when you know that you have invested in good companies and your original thesis for buying the stock(s) remains the same, a single down quarter or sporadic down quarters should be no reason to worry. What you should be looking for when reviewing 10Qs is **trends** over time. Let's say that the company has been reporting to be struggling for quite some time, maybe a few quarters in a row. In those circumstances, you can take a look at your original investment thesis and decide whether you want to keep the company in your portfolio or take a deeper dive into what exactly may be going on before deciding to sell it and move on.

Quarterly Reports usually come out during "earnings season" which is when most companies report earnings. You can easily find a 10Q in a public company official website under their "investor's relations" tab.

Lesson 31:
Earnings Season

Earnings season is the time during the year in which the vast majority of publicly traded companies report earnings. It happens 4 times per year (quarterly) and lasts for a few months or so until most companies have reported earnings.

During earnings season, public companies go over their annual or quarterly results in a conference call which is available to the public. Links for the full presentation, including how to listen live, can be found within the investor's relations section of a company's website. Within the same section, you can also find out when the next earnings announcement is if it hasn't already passed. To avoid any radical reactions from investors, earnings announcements usually happen before or after the market opens and not in the middle of a trading day.

Did you know – as a part-owner (or prospective part-owner) of a company, you are welcome to listen in on all earnings calls?! You can listen live as it is happening, listen to the recording and/or read the full transcript at your convenience once the call is over. Some investors/shareholders even have the chance to attend the event live. I've personally never done that but I think it's pretty awesome.

Lesson 32:
Investors Relations

Not too long ago, the only people that had access to financial reports, quarterly reports, annual reports, conference calls etc. were owners of companies, the wealthy and top brokers in Wall Street. These were the only ones with real access and authority to buy stocks for their clients.

Thankfully, in October 2000, the Security and Exchange Commission (SEC) passed "Regulation FD" or Fair Disclosure Regulation which made it possible for everyone to have access to information pertinent to a public entity. The idea is that anyone who wants to own "part" of a company through stock investing should be well aware of everything that the company has to offer. For that reason, any reports from publicly traded companies containing information that investors should know are readily available – and free. Documents include income statements, balance sheets, cash statements, annual reports, quarterly reports and beyond.

To find the section with all of the noted documents, simply go to the official website of the company that you may be interested in and look for a tab that says "investor relations". Another way to find it is through a simple Google search: "[company name] investor's relations" and that particular section should promptly appear in the search results.

You'll be able to find a wealth of information that can allow you to make better investment decisions. Any information that should be public but isn't can get a company in trouble. If officials of public companies hide information that the SEC believes should be public, they can be accused of insider trading which, as you may have heard, is illegal and comes with significant consequences.

Public information helps everyone have a more even playing field when it comes to investing in companies.

Lesson 33:
Annual Reports (10K)

A 10k is an **annual** report (as opposed to quarterly, which we discussed in a previous lesson). Think of a 10k as an annual (full year) "report card" which publicly traded companies release for investors. As you may expect, this report is much more comprehensive than a 10Q and is hundreds of pages long.

The role of this extensive report is to provide shareholders (and prospective investors) with information about anything that they may want to know regarding the internal operations of a specific company.

In the annual report, you can find information about everything from the business (what the company does, its various products, how long it's been around), to its risks (things to look out for if you are thinking about investing in that company) and all the way to relevant financial information for the entire year as compared with previous years and company strategies and expectations for years going forward. You can also find information about the management and tons of additional data.

You can find annual reports for multiple years within the investor's relations section of a company's website (as previously mentioned). You can also find it through "EDGAR", a subdivision of the Securities and Exchange Commission which is in charge of housing all required documents from publicly traded companies. Or, as always, you can simply do a Google search: "[company name], 10K" or "[company name], annual report" and see what comes up.

Remember: All of these reports are free and available to the public. Furthermore, 10K, 10Q and financial data are only available for companies that are publicly traded and have stocks available for the public. This information is usually not available for private companies.

Lesson 34:
Diversification – What It Is And Why It's Important

You may have heard the sayings "it's good to diversify" and "don't put all your eggs in one basket". What does this really mean? In the investing world, to diversify a portfolio can mean various things and can involve international companies, bonds, ETFs, Mutual Funds etc. For this particular lesson, we will focus solely on what it means to build a diversified portfolio of U.S. Stocks.

There are thousands of companies that are publicly traded and with that come the various sectors or industries in which said companies operate in. Top sectors within the U.S. economy include Consumer discretionary, Consumer Staples, Energy, Financials, Industrials, Information Technology, Materials, Telecommunication services and Utilities.

When we talk about diversifying your portfolio, we talk about the idea that your portfolio should be composed of different companies in different sectors or industries. Why is this a good idea? Well, diversifying allows you to cut down on risks tremendously by allowing your portfolio to have balance. If one industry or company is suffering, for instance, you can have peace of mind in that the other companies in your portfolio should be doing just fine. Let's say you own an assortment of companies in different industries – consumer goods, technology, industrials and utilities – you have a much well-balanced portfolio and your risk won't be as large as having "all your eggs in one basket".

This also applies to whether you have a 401(K) at the company where you work. You should never put all your money in your company's stock because anything could happen. For example, if your company goes bankrupt, the stocks in your portfolio that are tied to the business will go with it as well. Ever heard of "Enron"? A quick Google search can refresh your memory. The short story is that employees that had their entire retirement tied to Enron stock were left with nothing at the end of the day when the business went into bankruptcy. By working at your company, you are already "invested" in the business solely by the fact that you are an employee there. Try to diversify and choose other investments where you can put your money. With that said, it is okay to have some money invested where you work, but don't get carried away!

Lesson 35:
Capital Gains Taxes

In a nutshell, capital gains refer to the money that you make from an investment. There are two kinds of capital gains – short-term and long-term. You make capital gains every time you sell your stocks for more than you bought them, making a profit. Also, every time a company that you part-own pays you a dividend. Capital gains tax depends on various factors and, as you may know, taxes can get a bit complicated depending on every individual situation. And thus, in this lesson, my goal is to provide you with a ***general*** idea of how much you should expect to get taxed for the money made from your investments. *Remember to always consult your tax professional when it comes to managing your personal tax situation.*

Uncle Sam absolutely encourages and rewards when individuals invest for the long term. In the tax world, "long term" means owning your stock for at least 12 months or longer. Any investment that is bought and sold in less than a year is considered a short-term investment. The longer you hold your stocks, the less your capital gains tax and vice versa.

Not everyone is taxed the same when it comes to investments and percentages may change every year depending on IRS standards on how much you money make. Hence, regardless of when you are reading this book, make sure to check for appropriate percentages. As per the official IRS website, here are the 2015 general guidelines for long term gains:

Single			Tax rate on qualified dividends and long term capital gains
		to	
	$0	$9,225	0%
	$9,225	$37,450	0%
	$37,450	$90,750	15%
	$90,750	$189,300	15%
	$189,300	$411,500	15%
	$411,500	$413,200	15%
	$413,200	+	20%
Married filing jointly			
		to	
	$0	$18,450	
	$18,450	$74,900	0%
	$74,900	$151,200	0%
	$151,200	$230,450	15%
	$230,450	$411,500	15%
	$411,500	$464,850	15%
	$464,850	+	20%

For further info check out **IRS.GOV**

In order to determine how much you may be expected to pay in taxes once you start your investing journey (or if you already started), identify how much you make on the left-hand side and on the right-hand side you can see how much in taxes you should expect to pay if you hold your stocks for a year or longer. As noted, the longer you hold on to your investments, the less you get taxed. The taxes on short-term capital gains usually start at 20% (depending on your income) and move up from there.

Lesson 36:
What Is A Stock Split?

If you have shares of a company that experiences a stock split, nothing much changes financially. You technically own "more shares" of the company but at a lesser price. Again, this doesn't change anything on your investing account other than the number of shares you see and the price. I'll explain using Netflix as an example.

On 7/15/2015, Netflix went from $690 per share to around $98 per share in one day. What happened? The stock split seven ways, also called a 7:1 split. In other words, if you owned one share of Netflix before the split at $690, then after the split you owned 7 shares at $98 each!

Why do companies do this? For various reasons, but a big one is that sometimes companies want to attract more shareholders and create more liquidity. A price of almost $700 a share may seem intimidating to most people wanting to invest in Netflix while $100 maybe not so much. Remember, this is all "psychological" as nothing regarding the core value of the business has changed.

Although this doesn't happen for all companies that split, Netflix stock price actually increased about 16% in just 3 days after the split. One main reason for this is that they also reported a successful quarter which added onto the hype and boosted the stock price. However, remember to never invest in a stock that splits simply because you hope it will experience a rapid increase in price. A significant increase in stock price after a split is not the norm.

Note: There is also something called a "reverse split" where companies do the complete opposite. Let's say the stock price is $2.50 and a company may do a 5:1 reverse split where the price turns to $12.50. Reverse splits are quite rare but is still something you should know!

Netflix is not a recommendation, simply an example for this lesson.

Lesson 37:
Fundamental Analysis

Investors that use fundamental analysis for their decisions focus on researching the intrinsic (real value) of a company by digging deep into financial and business statements. In this case, the investor wants to find out whether they can get a great company at a great value and/or whether the company is a bit "overpriced", depending on the findings.

The main documents reviewed by fundamentally-focused investors include income statements, balance sheets, statement of cash flows, annual reports (10K), quarterly reports (10Q), information about the company's history as well as future growth prospects, valuation and more. Basically, the investor wants to make sure that they make a well-educated decision about what they are buying.

As an investor, my strategy consists of taking a very close look and analysis of the noted documents before making a decision. Although the noted research may seem very time-consuming, the truth is that the more it's done, the easier it gets. With practice, you'll soon develop the skill of knowing what is relevant – what matters, what doesn't and what to focus on. So, don't let it scare you.

Lesson 38:
Technical Analysis

Technical analysis differs from fundamental analysis in that it uses statistical data to provide investors with information that can predict fluctuations within stock prices over short time periods. Individuals that focus on technical analysis don't really care about the fundamental/intrinsic value of a company. Instead, they focus on patterns within stock charts in order to make investing decisions. For example, chart patterns can tell a technical-focused trader which is the best time to buy the stock and when to "jump out" and sell. People that focus on this method usually hold their shares for less than 24 hours as they are usually just buying and selling over and over again (remember that every time you buy and sell something, your online broker takes a fee, so this can become expensive).

I personally don't participate in technical analysis and never have. The "downfall" of this method is that most investors are not looking at the fundamentals of the companies. Instead, they are simply looking for patterns on a chart that would tell them when to buy and sell. With that said, there are people out there that know how to do this well. People have their different ways of making money in the market and I respect everyone's strategy. Investing is a very personal endeavor and you have to feel comfortable and confident with your approach. What makes me feel confident, comfortable and profitable is being a long-term value investor and buying stocks as if I were buying the company. You have to know yourself well!

Lesson 39:
What Is Gross Margin?

As most of us can probably agree, revenue (aka sales) is obviously extremely important when it comes to evaluating the financial health of a business. You want to know that the business is making money and that sales are growing year over year at a healthy pace.

However, keep in mind that it is very possible for a business to make tons of sales yet spend all of their money in the production of the goods sold (or services offered) and have nothing left over to pay bills and other obligations – including giving money back to shareholders. That means the company has a deficit and that wouldn't work for us as intelligent investors!

So, how do you find out if a company is producing enough money to meet ALL of its obligations and still have plenty left over? That brings us to this topic: **Gross Margin.**

In a nutshell, gross margin represents the percentage of sales that a company is able to keep after incurring the direct costs associated with producing the goods and/or services they provide to their customers. The number can be found in a company's income statement and it is in a percentage form. The higher the percentage number, the more the business is able to retain per each dollar of sales to cover costs and other obligations.

Here is the formula to find gross margin:

> Gross Margin (%) = (Revenue − Cost of Goods Sold)/Revenue

Good news: If you thought you had to sit down and calculate it on your own, guess what — you don't have to! Most companies calculate it and have it readily available for all investors. All you need to do is take a peak into the financial statements section of any quarterly report or annual report for a company. You can also check websites such as [Yahoo! Finance](#) or [Morningstar](#) for this kind of data.

Here is an example:

Let's say Company X had **revenue** (sales) of $1 million dollars from selling their popular skates, apparel and whatever other goods they sell. Let's suppose it **cost** them $500,000 to produce all of those goods that they made and sold to the public. In this very simple example, we can calculate that Company X has a **gross margin** of 50%. That means the business is able to retain $0.50 for every $1 of sales that they make. The extra money is used to cover bills, pay shareholders and invest back into the company.

Lesson 40:
Direct Stock Purchase Plans And Transfer Agents: Explained

A Direct Stock Purchase Plan or Transfer Agent is the division of a publicly traded corporation that allows you to buy shares of stock directly through the company itself instead of using an online brokerage account. You can simply contact the company's transfer agent directly and let them know that you'd like to buy some shares.

Some companies have minimums in terms of how many shares you can buy through their Direct Purchase Plans. Most don't usually allow you to contact them for one single share. You may be required to either enroll in a bi-weekly or monthly feature where money from your preferred bank account is deducted and invested in the company depending on the time frame you choose. Or, you may be simply asked to invest a lump sum.

One benefit of a Direct Purchase Plan as opposed to using an online brokerage account is that most (if not all) won't charge any recurring fees and/or any initial fees to start may be very minimal. For example, some may have a one-time payment of $20 or charge only $1 to enroll in a plan. Most online brokers will charge you anywhere from $4.95 to $9.99 and beyond when buying/selling shares, so the transfer agent/direct purchase fees could be a lot cheaper in comparison.

One "downside" is that, if you have multiple companies in mind that you want to invest in, you'll have to deal with multiple transfer agents and getting paperwork from everywhere as opposed to having your portfolio all in one place, which is what an online broker offers.

Not all publicly traded companies have transfer agents but most do. The easiest way to find out whether a company that you want to invest in has this option is simply to Google: "[company name] transfer agent" and the information will likely come right up. Another way is to click on the "investor's relations" tab or section on the website of the business that you are interested in and search for "transfer agent" or "direct purchase plans" on that page. There should either be a phone number for you to call directly or some kind of form that you can fill out. Remember to always find the transfer agent information on a company's official website in order to avoid any scams.

Some examples of popular companies that allow you to invest directly through them include Nike, Disney, Starbucks, Apple, Coca-Cola – the list goes on. Note: several of the major publicly traded companies use a service called "Computershare" which manages their direct purchase plans division. I am mentioning this in case you see that name show up in your research.

Lesson 41:
What Does It Mean To Short A Stock? Is It Worth It?

Investors who decide to "short" a stock are investors who may feel that the price of a particular stock is too expensive and expect the price to decrease notably within a set period of time.

Investors make money from shorting by virtually "borrowing" a number of shares from their online brokerage accounts (shares they don't really own) and selling them to someone who wants them in the market at that particular high price. If the price of the stock does, in fact, end up falling, the investor that made that "bet" ends up with the difference between the "high price" and the price to which the stock fell to. If, on the other hand, the stock price stays high and doesn't fall in price within the necessary time period, the investor that predicted that the price would fall would be responsible to "cover their short", meaning, pay for the difference in those shares to the online broker – this time with their own money.

General Example: You feel that **AZ Corporation** stock price is too high, currently trading at $670 per share. You want to "short" ten shares of AZ Corp stock and you make the transaction with your online broker indicating that the stock price will fall to $500 within the next 2 months. If the stock price, in fact, falls to the designated amount, the shorter of the stock gets to keep that difference in price: $1,700 (670-500 = 170 x 10= $1,700). They get to keep that money without doing anything other than making that "bet" with the money from the online broker. If, however, AZ Corp price doesn't go down to $500 and, instead, keeps rising, the person shorting the stock will owe the online broker that $1,700 and won't have any stocks to speak of. In investing lingo, this is called "covering their short".

The high risk that comes with shorting is the fact that you are investing on margin. This means that you are using stocks and money that doesn't belong to you but to the online brokerage account.

My personal opinion on this is that shorting stocks is a very risky and aggressive investment strategy. This is an approach to investing that I'd personally never take. The truth is that we never know what a particular stock or the stock market as a whole will do. So, making bets on assumptions – especially when you are using money that is not yours – is never a good idea. High-quality, straight-forward, long-term value investing is never that complicated and much less risky. Keep that in mind!

Lesson 42:
What Happens When A Stock You Own Goes "Bankrupt"?

When a company files bankruptcy, they can go about it in two ways – the business will either file for reorganization of the business (chapter 11 or 13 bankruptcy) or they can file for liquidation (chapter 7 bankruptcy).

In *reorganization*, the business, with the help of the assigned bankruptcy clerk, will do everything it can possibly do to bring the business back to life. For instance, it will make agreements and payment deals with vendors and clients, will sell some assets in order to pay off some debt, will lay off workers, among other recommended strategies. If the reorganization process is not successful, however, the business proceeds with the *liquidation* chapter which involves getting rid of all assets within the company and dissolving the business in its entirety. If the business in question is a publicly traded company (meaning it sells stocks), the stock price will usually also start decreasing significantly and may reach $0.

As a company is going out of business, the respective exchange in which the stock trades (i.e. New York Stock Exchange, Nasdaq, etc.) will have its own individual rules for ultimately delisting the stock from the respective exchange. As clearly outlined on the Security & Exchange Commission website:

"...After a company's stock starts trading on an exchange, it usually is subject to other, less stringent requirements; if it fails

to meet those, the stock can be delisted. As with listing requirements, the standards for delisting shares are not uniform; each exchange has its own requirements." Source

Getting delisted means that the ticker symbol or company name will no longer appear on the exchange in which it trades because no one is able to buy or sell the stock any longer.

If you bought the stock on "margin", meaning that you used borrowed money from the online broker to buy your shares, then you will still owe that money to the broker (the money you borrowed) regardless of the fact that the company is no longer in operation. This is one of the reasons why I discourage investors (regardless of their expertise in the stock market) from trading or investing on margin.

On the other hand, ***if you bought the stock using your own money*** and the stock goes to zero, the only thing you can lose is the money you invested. The company that went bankrupt, nor its customers or vendors or anyone they did business with can come after you for anything. Your responsibility only goes as far as how much money you had invested in the company and that's where it ends. When it comes to investing, the lowest point you can go is "zero" (you won't owe anyone anything if you buy shares with your own money). However, the highest you can go has no limit – which is pretty awesome!

Remember that you can also choose to invest in **index funds** which have the advantage of being composed of various companies and usually follow whatever happens in the market. In theory, an index fund could never go to zero unless ALL the companies within the index fund go out of business – which is nearly impossible. *A bit more about index funds in part two of this book.*

Lesson 43:
How Long Investors Have To Wait To See A Return On Stock Investments

Two Words: **It depends!**

- How much money you start with (i.e. how much money you allocate to a particular company which is tied to how many shares you buy).

- Overall performance of the company and its effect on the stock price

Remember: Always think long term

Examples:

Let's use Coca-Cola (NYSE: KO) as a general example.

One share of Coca-Cola currently trades at $43.29 (as of December 4th 2015).
Let's say that you bought 50 shares of Coca-Cola **5 years ago** (December 3rd 2010) when the stock price was $27.85 per share at the total cost of ~$1392.50.

Over those 5 years, Coca-Cola stock price has appreciated **~55%**
This means that you would have ~$2,158.37 in your investing account (your original investment of $1392 would have grown to over $2,000 based on the performance of the stock over those five years).

***

Taking it back to **10 year ago**, when Coca-Cola stock price was $15.96

You would have been able to buy 50 shares for the grand total of $798
Over the last 10 years the stock has appreciated ~**171%**
This means that you would have ~**$2,162.58** (your initial investment of $798 would have grown to over $2,000 based on the performance of the stock over those 10 years)

The noted returns on investment don't even take into account the **dividends** (which is additional money that Coca-Cola gives shareholders every 3 months). Hence, the total return on investment would actually be more than what is shown here.

And there you have it! As you can see, time horizon plays a significant role on how much your money grows if you invest in a high-quality company. In a general sense, the longer the money has to grow, the better it is for your investment portfolio. This is why I feel it is so important to develop the traits and attitude of a *long-term value investor* and I cannot stress that enough!

Remember: Historical performance of a company is **NEVER** a guarantee of future performance. Anything can happen to a business or the stock market as a whole at any time. Nobody has a crystal ball which is why it is so important to do our homework (research!) before buying shares in any company. The available information that we analyze can give us a generally good idea of where a business is headed in the future. However, remember that there are no guarantees. Stocks have ongoing fluctuations so it is important to keep thinking long term and let your money work for you over time.

*The listed company is not a recommendation. Simply an example used to bring the point across.

Lesson 44:
When To Sell A Stock

"Our favorite holding period is forever."
– Warren Buffett

As long-term value investors, meaning we are meant to hold our stocks for an indefinite amount of time, many people wonder when it's a good idea to sell a stock. There are many reasons why an individual would want to sell their shares. The goal with long-term value investing is to do a good amount of research up-front, invest in good-quality companies that are the crème of the crop within their industries (and with strong growth potential) and to see them grow over time.

However, it is also good to keep in mind that perhaps holding something "forever" may be a bit unrealistic. Here I will share what I have learned from experience regarding the top three good reasons why it may be a good idea to sell a stock in your portfolio:

1. Your original investment thesis has changed significantly. Remember one of the prior lessons where I outlined the importance of writing down an investment plan? Well, if the original thesis for why you bought the stock has changed significantly into something you don't quite understand, this should be a red flag. Also, if you no longer have a clear picture of how things will work out in the long term, leaving you lost and confused, that would be a good time to consider selling perhaps a portion of your shares or all of them if it is warranted.

2. Competition is heating up. Keep your eyes peeled for up-and-coming and fierce competition, at all times! As we all know, competition can sneak up on any company at any time so it is important to stay aware. Read every article and/or analyst report that you can get your hands on about the company that you are interested in and notice whether they are talking a lot about a particular competitor and/or any significant threats to the business.

3. You've had a very good run and have a better idea of where to put your money. Often times you don't want to just sell to sell. Perhaps you've come across a new company that seems to have strong prospects and you have done your research. Also, remember that "cash is king", so even if you sell and you want to keep that money in cash until you come across another "great" opportunity, it is totally okay to do that as well.

Lesson 45:
Socially Responsible Investing

Although various investors may have their own interpretation of this particular concept, at its very core, socially responsible investing (SRI) is the idea of investing only in companies that provide products or services that are good for the environment, people and the world as a whole. A socially responsible investor would likely stay away from any stocks or companies that derive their profits from selling tobacco, alcohol, or other substances that may be considered addictive and/or harmful for individuals in the long term. SRIs may also stay away from companies that produce fumes or gas that harm the environment, use child labor, or that test on animals, for example.

Whether or not the business is for profit or non-profit is irrelevant to SRI – the question always is whether or not what the business sells harms the world.

Some examples of companies that socially responsible investors may avoid include:

Altria Group (NYSE: MO) – Parent company of Marlboro and other brands of cigarettes or smokeless tobacco, as well as wine products.

Monsanto Company (NYSE: MON) – Agricultural producer and leader in the production of genetically modified foods (GMOs) and artificial flavors. As you may deduct, they are mostly disliked by advocates of organic food production.

The above are just a couple of examples but there are many companies out there that may bring up questions for the investor of whether or not they are socially responsible. Some investors may decide to stay away while there are others who don't really care about the debate of whether the business is socially responsible or not, as long as they make good money for investors.

The issue with this particular concept or idea is that, although it may be easy to identify some businesses as socially responsible, for other businesses the line may not be so clear. Some individuals can also take this concept or idea to an extreme. For example, some may also look to include fast-food restaurants and/or soda distributors, while others may not agree with that. The bottom line is that SRI is a concept that needs to be determined by each individual based on their own personal beliefs about what kind of businesses are harmful to the world and which businesses help it. Investors also have to determine whether this is a factor they want to include in their investment decisions or not.

Here are some questions to think about – what is your personal definition of socially responsible investing? If you can make a lot of money from a stock that possibly harms people and/or the environment (maybe even indirectly) would you still invest in that kind of company? If you discover that your favorite brand of handbags or shoes uses child labor to make those products, would you immediately switch brands and never invest in those businesses?

These are just some of the questions that can help clarify your position in this subject.

Lesson 46:
How To Prepare Yourself To Start Investing {Five Simple Steps}

I hope that all the lessons outlined in this book have provided you with a more solid understanding of the stock market, how it works and how you can benefit. You should now be ready to take small steps towards your investing journey. Below are some general guidelines to get started:

1. Set up an Investing Account and Save, Save, Save. If you are very new to investing and are just starting out, I recommend setting up an investing account which means that you start a savings account solely for the money that you plan to use for investing. Remember that money you designate for the stock market should be money that you won't need for the next 3-5+ years and beyond. Remember that long-term value investing means creating wealth over time by becoming part-owners of amazing companies. Start by putting aside $10, $100, $1,000 a month or whatever your budget allows after your core obligations. Be consistent with those savings for at least 6 months to one year.

2. Educate yourself as much as possible. As you save money every month, I recommend that you continue getting educated on the subject and familiarizing yourself with the world stocks and investing. Read books, find resources online, go to your local library and find issues of the Wall Street Journal (I used to do this all the time), listen to podcasts, take classes. Knowledge is power and the more you educate yourself the more comfortable you will feel about becoming an investor and buying your own pieces of great companies.

3. Start keeping a watch-list & researching companies you are interested in. A watch-list can be a simple piece of paper, notebook, or Excel spreadsheet on your computer where you start keeping track of companies that catch your attention and that you'd like to invest in one day. I also recommend writing down the stock price of the company when you first look at it. You'd be surprised as to how much prices go up, down, or stay indifferent over the course of a few months or a few years.

4. Research online brokerage accounts and pick one that suits your needs. There are tons of online brokerage accounts as previously mentioned. Check out the most popular ones and what kinds of fees they charge. Keep track of the ones that you come across for future reference. Also, make sure they are insured by the SIPC.

5. Just do it! The best way to learn is to start doing. Don't be afraid. Whether it's buying stocks or life in general the best way to get over fear and/or intimidation is through action! Start slow and small and work your way up from there.

Alternate Forms of Investing
(Outside of stocks)

ETFs: Exchange Trade Funds

In the world of investing, you will come across various options of where to put your money – from individual stocks and index funds to ETFs and beyond. It is important for you to understand what all these investment vehicles mean and how they differ from each other. In this particular mini-lesson, we will take a closer look at the difference between ETFs and individual stocks.

You can think of ETFs (Exchange Traded Funds) as a "packaged" investment made up of companies from specific industries or businesses. These days you can easily find ETFs focused around pretty much anything that you can think of including technology and consumer goods companies, dividend-paying companies, market indexes, sectors and even international investments. By purchasing an ETF, investors have the advantage of owning various pieces of companies from their sector/industry of interest in one single "package". ETFs are highly liquid – which means that you can buy and sell them any day that the market is open, similar to what you can do with stocks.

Examples:

The Vanguard Dividend Appreciation Index ETF (VIG) only includes companies that have been raising their dividend consistently for the past 10 years. Some of the top companies included within this ETF include Microsoft, Johnson & Johnson, Coca-Cola, Procter & Gamble, PepsiCo, among others. Sectors covered within the ETFs include consumer defensive, industrial, healthcare and technology.

First Trust Dow Jones Internet ETF (FDN) is an ETF composed of top companies from the technology and e-commerce industry. Some of the top holdings within this particular ETF include Amazon, Apple, Facebook, Netflix and Alphabet

(Google). FDN is known as the largest technology dedicated ETF in the market.

Changing gears into individual stocks: Remember, when you buy stocks, you are becoming a part-owner of one single company (as opposed to a "package" of companies). For example, if you buy stock in Coca-Cola, you own a small piece of Coca-Cola and that's it. Same goes for all other companies that offer individual stocks – you can choose to own shares of Facebook, Apple, or Netflix *individually* as opposed to owning them through an ETF.

Some investors may feel that ETFs are a bit "safer" in comparison to owning one single stock because they allow you to own multiple companies in one so that the risk is more widespread. However, this is not a rule by any means and it all depends on the quality of your investments – regardless of the type. Furthermore, one caveat to consider is that, if one of the companies from your ETF goes up 40% in one year, you will not benefit fully from that 40% increase because there are other investments in that ETF. And so, your return will be an *average* of the performance of ALL the businesses within that "package" and not from one single stock. Note that, although I am very familiar with ETFs, I have never bought or sold those types of investments. My experience has been solely with individual stocks.

Remember the noted company and ETFs are simply examples. Not recommendations.

Mutual Funds

You can think of a mutual fund as an investing vehicle composed of stocks, bonds, or a combination of the two. Think of a group of people putting their investing money together and deciding that they want to own pieces of various companies. The fund manager takes that money and buys a combination of different investing securities such as bonds and stocks, as noted. Finally, each person that invested gets a "piece" of that mutual fund.

Investors make money from mutual funds pretty much in the same way that they make money from stocks:

- *Dividends:* If the companies within the mutual fund pay a dividend, each investor will get his/her portion of the dividends depending on how much of the mutual fund they own. This is called a "distribution".

- *Capital Gains:* If the stocks within the mutual fund increase in price, investors get the difference between how much the stocks originally cost when purchased and how much they have increased in price over time. If an investor decides to sell their position in the mutual fund, they get their share of the profits.

Similar to the ETFs, which we previously discussed, mutual funds provide diversification which means that an investor can be a part-owner of different types of investments at once. Diversification is important because it provides a "cushion" or makes an investment less risky considering everything is not concentrated in one single stock or a single type of investment.

One downside of mutual funds to consider is the amount of fees they charge. Mutual funds are actively managed by a fund manager(s) who collect a paycheck, and thus, they may charge high fees for simply watching the mutual fund and/or making changes to the kinds of holdings the mutual fund has. The mutual fund manager will buy or sell and make changes according to what they feel would be best for the fund without the consent of the investors.

Historically speaking, other kinds of investment including stocks and index funds have provided a higher return on investment than mutual funds over time. Part of the reason for this is that a lot of the returns generated by mutual funds are "eaten up" by the fees involved. It is important to take a close look at management fees and expense ratios before investing in mutual funds.

Index Funds

You can think of an index fund as a security composed of various stocks from different industries and whose performance follows the performance of major stock indexes such as the S&P 500, NASDAQ or the Dow Jones.

[**The S&P 500** is an index composed of the 500 largest companies in the U.S representing the leading industries including industrial, technology, energy, materials, consumer goods, financials, consumer staples and utilities. Index funds are composed of the top companies & businesses in those industries.]

So basically, let's say that you choose to invest in an index fund which follows the S&P 500 (in other words, follows "the overall market") that particular investment you made will only increase or decrease depending on the performance of the market. If the overall market decreases in value, so will your investment. If the market flies high, so will your investment. Considering that there is not much "management" to do since the index fund follows whatever the market does, management fees for index funds are very low in comparison to those of mutual funds. The benefit of index funds is that they provide broad market exposure and is a form of "passive" investing, meaning that there is not much to be done other than purchase it and let it ride in accordance to the market over a long period of time.

One of the main differences between index funds and individual stocks is the level of risk and return. While you can think of index funds as more conservative or passive, often times the performance of index funds lacks behind the performance of a high-quality individual stock that has outperformed the market significantly. Investing in index funds doesn't give you the advantage of benefiting from the stellar performance of an individual company that has had a great run over time. Below is a graph representative of what I am talking about. Notice the performance of companies like Amazon, Nike and Apple in comparison to the S&P500 index fund over the past five years.

The percentages you see are the percentage gains that an investor would have obtained from investing in the companies listed Vs. the S&P index:

With that said, there is absolutely nothing wrong about taking the more conservative route when it comes to investing and putting your money into index funds as opposed to individual stocks. As a matter of fact, index funds are actually phenomenal investments for beginner investors as they provide a broad exposure of various companies in the market and have a lower level of risk. At the end of the day, it is all up to you and your risk tolerance! You are the captain of your ship, or in this case, your stock portfolio!

Expense Ratios: A General Overview

If you have money in individual stocks, you don't have to worry about expense ratios because they don't exist in the world of individual stocks. However, if you plan to invest (or are currently invested) in any kind of fund including index funds, ETFs and/or mutual funds, this should be of interest to you.

In a nutshell, **expense ratios** are the costs that come with maintaining a fund. Using the mutual fund example, for instance – mutual funds are actively managed by assigned managers who have the responsibility of keeping a close eye on all of the securities/types of investments in the mutual fund. These managers have the duty of making decisions to rebalance the fund or making any other type of changes that they feel are necessary. Additional fees incurred during the maintenance of the fund include administrative expenses and investment advisory fees.

To determine the expense ratio for a fund, all of the applicable fees are added up and then divided by the amount of people invested in that particular fund. Investors don't pay this out of pocket – the fees are deducted from the overall asset value of the fund. The tricky part about expense ratios is that they are owed **regardless** of the fund's performance. So, for instance, let's say the fund performed poorly during the year and investors ended up losing money. The expense ratio still applies and won't be adjusted as a result of poor management or performance. The opposite is also true – if the fund did well, the expense ratio is still deducted.

On average, the expense ratios for mutual funds are a lot higher than any other kind of fund considering there is a "fund manager" involved who actively manages the fund, as previously noted. Index funds or ETFs don't necessarily have a fund manager because those kinds of investments simply follow indexes or follow whatever the market or a particular industry sector is doing. And so, there is not much management to be done.

What you should be looking to pay (on average):

While expense ratios vary, try to find funds that have high-quality performance over time and low fees. A reasonable rate for a ratio should be in the ballpark of 0.5% or lower ($50 for every $10,000 of assets within the fund). If you come across ratios in the range of 1.5%-2% (i.e. $150-$200 per $10K of assets) and beyond, be careful. It is possible for individuals to pay more in expense fees than their actual return on investment over time which would defeat the purpose of investing. So, keep a very close eye on that.

Final Thoughts

Thank you for reading. I hope you walk away from this book with a better understanding of how the market works and how you can benefit from it. Remember that there is no rush. The stock market is not going anywhere, so take your time to know yourself, understand your risk tolerance, how much you want to start with, what kind of companies you want to become a part owner of and whatever else you feel will make you an informed and educated investor. Also, remember that the only way to become an investor is to invest, so take action when you're ready. *Cheers to profits!*

Learn More and Keep in Touch!

Join our Investing Boot-Camp: A one-on-one coaching program for beginner investors. We walk you through the entire process of investing – from opening your first online brokerage account and funding it, to analyzing individual stocks and finding companies to invest in. Learn to build your very first stock portfolio!

For details regarding our next class and everything covered in the course, send an email to:
girlsonthemoney@gmail.com

OR

Teachmetoinvest@gmail.com

With the caption:

"Investing Course"

Find us on social Media!

Instagram: @girlsonthemoney
Facebook Page:
Facebook.com/girlsonthemoney
Private Facebook Group:
Facebook.com/groups/girlsonthemoney
Official Site: Girlsonthemoney.com

Made in the USA
Middletown, DE
22 December 2020